Fa

MW01136941

When Belief Is Hard

Steve Brown

New
Growth
Press

WWW.NEWGROWTHPRESS.COM

New Growth Press, Greensboro, NC 27404
www.newgrowthpress.com
Copyright © 2016 by Key Life

All Scripture quotations are taken from the *Holy Bible,
English Standard Version*®. Copyright © 2000; 2001 by
Crossway Bibles, a division of Good News Publishers. Used
by permission. All rights reserved.

Cover Design: Tandem Creative, Tom Temple,
tandemcreative.net
Typesetting: Lisa Parnell, lparnell.com

ISBN: 978-1-942572-35-0 (Print)
ISBN: 978-1-942572-36-7 (eBook)

Library of Congress Cataloging-in-Publication Data
    Names: Brown, Stephen W.
    Title: Faith and doubt : when belief is hard / Steve
Brown.
    Description: Greensboro, NC : New Grow Press, 2016. |
Includes bibliographical references and index.
    Identifiers: LCCN 2015038160 | ISBN 9781942572350
(print) | ISBN 9781942572367 (ebook)
    Subjects: LCSH: Faith.
    Classification: LCC BV4637 .B77 2016 | DDC
234/.23—dc23
    LC record available at http://lccn.loc.gov/2015038160

Printed in China

23 22 21 20 19 18 17 16   1 2 3 4 5

In Lewis Carroll's *Alice in Wonderland*, the Queen says she is a great age—"one hundred and one, five months and a day."

"I can't believe that!" said Alice.

"Can't you?" the Queen said in a pitying tone. "Try again: draw a long breath, and shut your eyes."

Alice laughed. "There's no use trying," she said, "one *can't* believe impossible things."

"I daresay you haven't had much practice," said the Queen. "When I was your age, I always did it for half-an-hour a day. Why, sometimes I believed as many as six impossible things before breakfast!"[1]

You may feel that way about faith.

I've noticed that there are different types of unbelief.

There are some who say about belief, "That's absolute nonsense." That's fine. Maybe they shouldn't waste their time with it at all.

There are others who say about belief, "I've never doubted. It's all true. My mother said it was true, I believe her, and my mother wouldn't lie." They are living in denial. That isn't real faith. They simply haven't yet hit the "rocks of reality." If you're in this category, we can talk when the time comes . . . when the doctor says you have cancer, when your teenage daughter is pregnant, when your life falls apart.

Then there are the others who really do believe . . . most of the time. You've given your life to this thing and there's no turning back. God has you and you're stuck. But sometimes in the dark, you think, *I hope this is true. I really hope I haven't just dreamed this up and wasted my life.*

This is for you. Here's some help for when it gets dark from John 10:22–42.

When Believing Is Hard and Pretending Doesn't Work

To start off, I have two important asides.

The first aside is this: Those spiritual giants who say they never doubt, never wonder, and never question are lying. They don't mean to do it, but they do. Those who have been Christians for a long time don't do any favors to new Christians when they pretend to believe without doubt. We all doubt and come from a long line of doubters. Mother Teresa honestly revealed her struggle with doubt in letters published after her death. Thomas Aquinas said "It is all straw," and Charles Spurgeon had long periods of depression. They all experienced doubt in the face of life's brokenness.

You might have heard the story of the two guys sitting together. One asked the other what he did for a living. He said he was a pastor. The man responded, "That's interesting. I keep my religion simple—Jesus loves me, this I know, for the Bible tells me so."

The pastor, in turn, asked the man what he did for a living. He said he was a professor of astronomy at the state university. The pastor responded, "I keep my astronomy simple—twinkle, twinkle, little star."

But of course astronomy isn't that easily understood. The gospel message is simple, yes: Jesus loves me, this I know, for the Bible tells me so. But what we believe is so astounding and gigantic that anyone who says they "just accept it" is crazy. The truth is, we believe some really big things.

The second aside: it's dumb to dumb-down doctrine to fit your doubt (John 10:33).

A friend of mine came to me once and said, "Steve, I have an orthodox rabbi who wants to talk to a Christian, but he said that he wants to talk to a *real* Christian . . . not one who calls himself a Christian but doesn't believe anything." That rabbi understood.

When I was a theological liberal, I didn't believe in the virgin birth because intellectuals know that virgins simply don't give birth. I didn't believe in the resurrection because intellectuals know that dead people simply don't get out of graves. I didn't believe all of the Bible was true because intellectuals are simply not that silly.

But then my daughter became seriously sick . . .

If the Christian faith isn't true, find out and get away from it because if you're faking it, there won't be enough faith to deal with your divorce, abuse, illness, many sins, and eventual death. It really is dumb to dumb-down your doctrine to fit your doubt.

Now to some biblical truths that can change your life.

I'm an old guy . . . and I'm still here. I shouldn't be here. I'm the biggest sinner I know. I have failed more times than I can say, and I have had doubts that you have never even thought up. But I'm still here. I know about doubt. I've been there, done that, and have several bloodied T-shirts to prove it. Here are some things I have learned about faith when my life has hit those rocks of reality. They are hard-won, simple, life-changing truths.

Hope Precedes Faith

Hope precedes faith and greases the tracks on which faith runs.

"So the Jews gathered around him and said to him, 'How long will you keep us in suspense? If you are the Christ, tell us plainly'" (John 10:24). While some of that may have been unbelief, I know people. For some of those people, that was not an expression of unbelief, but an expression of hope.

Then Jesus gives them the most amazing promises, "I give them eternal life, and they will never perish, and no one will snatch them out of my hand" (John 10:28).

Do you want to live forever? Do you want to be accepted? Do you want to be forgiven? Do you want to be loved? *Why?*

Where did you get those desires? Your hopes come from him. If you're hungry, that may mean there is food. If you're thirsty, that may mean there is water. If you hope for eternal life, acceptance, forgiveness, and love, it may mean it exists and can be yours.

I once conducted a skeptics' forum in a church I was serving. I was the only Christian present, and skeptics came and asked their questions. I remember one woman who started to cry after hearing about Jesus. She said, "Oh God, I wish this were true."

It is dumb to dumb-down your doctrine to fit your doubt. It is also dumb to dumb-down your hope to fit your low expectations.

Your hopes are a gift from God. Your hopes are an indication that God is there and your hope is not in vain.

Intentionality Magnifies Faith

Intentionality magnifies faith and strengthens the foundation on which faith rests (John 10:31–39). Belief isn't something that just happens. Belief and unbelief are both intentional.

Why do I say that? Consider this: you may not want to believe because it irritates you that you can't be God. There is one God, and you're not him. As long as there is a God, you can't be in charge. I don't want to be negative, but if that's the case, forget about faith. You simply can't get there from here.

You may not want to believe because you're afraid that God will send you to the Middle East or Africa or something. I don't want to be negative, but if that's the case, forget about faith. You simply can't get there from here.

You may not want to believe because you like sleeping with your girlfriend (or boyfriend), engaging in less than honest business practices, or lying about who you are. I don't want to be negative, but if that's the case, forget about faith. You simply can't get there from here . . . not because you aren't obedient, but because you don't want him to be Lord.

You may not want to believe because you're afraid your friends will think you're a fanatic. I don't want to be negative, but if that's the case, forget about faith. You simply can't get there from here.

On the other hand, if you want to believe—if you *really* want to believe no matter what—you will because you are, even now, making that choice. You choose to believe or not.

According to Augustine, the world says that seeing is believing but God says that believing is seeing. Let me show you how this works. Right now God is doing stuff in your life because he likes you, but generally when God does something, there is an alternate explanation and you get to choose. For example, when you pray that your child will be healed and your child recovers after going to the doctor, you can either believe that God used medicine to heal your child, or you can believe that you didn't need God at all. If you choose the second explanation, God won't be angry and he will still like you, but your faith won't get watered and it may become sick. However, if you see God's hand in everything about your life, acknowledge his hand, and praise him for it; it will feed your faith and make it strong.

Facts Enhance Faith

Facts enhance faith and confirm the direction God has established (John 10:37–38). Apologetics (the defense of the faith) wins arguments because the facts justify the reality.

Many people who aren't Christians are not willing to check out the facts of the faith because they are afraid that God might be there and they don't want him to be. But here is the strange thing: a lot of Christians don't check out the facts of the faith because they are afraid that God might not be there. They don't read books, ask questions, or entertain doubts because it is better to hope that the Christian faith is true than it is to check it out and find out that it isn't true.

Do you know the good thing about being old and religious? I've read all the books, asked all the questions, and doubted all the doubts . . . and I know it is true. Go ahead and check it out. It's true.

I have friends who are a married couple. The wife came to me for counseling and thought her husband was having an affair. He wasn't. I had talked to him and then checked. I said to her, "Why don't you just hire a private detective and find out?" She said, "I can't do that." I replied, "Then continue to doubt."

I've counseled many people with doubts. When I suggest that they buy some books, ask questions, and check out those who doubt and those who believe to find out which is credible, I often get in response, "I can't do that." Again I say, "Then continue to doubt."

C. S. Lewis said that he came to faith by using the logic taught by his atheist professors. The facts are there. Check them out.

Trust Affirms Faith

Trust affirms faith and creates the soft place where faith rests (John 10:27–30). Do you struggle with doubt? Like most things that have to do with our faith, God has you covered.

Obsessive-compulsive faith will kill you and leave you in a joyless struggle with unbelief. Some people think they can't be Christians because they are still sinners, so they are obsessed with their sins. But don't you realize that Jesus came for sinners? So you don't need to be obsessive about your purity.

Are you struggling with sin? Are you trying very, very hard not to sin? Martin Luther would say to you, "If you sin, sin boldly." He didn't say that to give you license to sin, he said it because he knew that you, just like everyone else, are going to sin. And God has provided a safety net, Jesus, the Friend of sinners who has paid it all and done it all. Don't worry about your sins. Instead, confess them and forget them (1 John 1:8–9).

Some people are also obsessive about how much faith they have. They are afraid that they don't have "enough" faith. When John Wesley said that he couldn't preach faith because he didn't have faith, Peter Böhler told him, "Preach faith till you have it; and then, because you have it, you will preach faith."

Are you struggling with faith? Quit obsessing over it. Just make a list of how you would live if you really believed. When you have faith, you will live that way because you have it.

This stuff is true, so relax and live like it is. You don't believe in order to belong to Jesus. You believe because you already do.

How Can I Be Assured of My Salvation?

Quite often, the Christian who struggles with the assurance of his or her salvation is actually struggling with feelings versus facts. You may not feel like a Christian; however, if you have accepted Jesus Christ, then the fact is your salvation is secure and sure. Not only that, the fact is that you are loved, forgiven, and accepted by the God of the universe.

You may not feel God's presence. While it may be frustrating for us, from our human perspective, God usually meets Christians with only "a still, small voice," if that. The problem is, we expect God to meet us instead in grand, emotional, and miraculous ways. At those times of struggle, it's helpful to remember 1 Kings 19:11–12.

> And he said, "Go out and stand on the mount before the LORD." And behold, the LORD passed by, and a great and strong wind tore the mountains and broke in pieces the rocks before the LORD, but the LORD was not in the wind. And after the wind an earthquake, but the LORD was not in the earthquake. And after the earthquake a fire, but the LORD was not in the fire. And after the fire the sound of a low whisper.

Of course, the voice of the Lord was in the low whisper.

When we question God's work in our life, the assurance of our salvation, and the implications of faith, sometimes that question reflects a classic Christian problem—the problem of missing the clear teaching of the New Testament on God's grace made possible in Jesus Christ. There is no way to "fall off the path," simply because God's grace and love for you is a settled fact.

Grace is a function of God's love; it is not based on our actions or behavior. As Christians, we have been called to live in the freedom of Christ—his gift to us. The fact is, as hard as it is to accept at certain times, Christ has already paid for our sin, struggles, and guilt. Shame should lead us back to God, but it often causes us to turn from him.

As a Christian, your natural desire is to please God—even when you continue to mess up and struggle—not because he will punish you if you don't please him, but because of his great love for you. The point is this: our obedience comes from freedom, not freedom from obedience.

Remember that no one is always content or happy or even aware of God's work in his or her life. Aside from yours, mine, and others' actual lives right now, the Bible is full of examples—David in the Psalms, Job, and Paul, among others. The problem with being human is that so often our feelings (or lack of them) get in the way. So if I don't feel like a Christian today, if I don't feel joyous today, if I don't feel loving today, if I don't feel God's presence today, then it must follow that I'm not living my life as a Christian and something must be wrong. That mistaken thinking is just not true. Just because you don't feel a certain way today has nothing to do with the facts—of God's presence, of his acceptance, love, and forgiveness, or of your salvation.

The problem of depending on our feelings to assess our faith is especially true if we're in the midst of pain, stress, or trouble. This tends to directly "color" our view of life and that, in turn, affects our relationship with God. Other things affect our relationship with God—our relationships with our family (especially with our parents), past issues, physical pain, job problems, anxiety, depression, and the like.

Let me ask you a few questions: If you knew you were forgiven, no matter what, would you then find the joy restored? If you knew that God loved you and accepted you, no matter what, would you then be free? If you knew that you belonged to God and he would never let you go, no matter what, would it be easier to worship and serve him as Lord?

If you answered yes to those three questions, then your problem is solved. Why? Because if you are a Christian, you are forgiven. You are loved and accepted. You belong to God and he will never let you go. Check out the following Scriptures (among others): Matthew 11:28–29; John 10:27–30; Romans 8:1–2; 8:28–39; Philippians 1:6; 1 Thessalonians 5:23–24 as well as 1 John 1:9.

When Christians struggle with the assurance of their salvation, it reminds me of a swimmer who is drowning. The more that swimmer flails his arms and legs in a desperate attempt to save his life, the closer he comes to drowning. Instead, if the swimmer were just to relax and let the water hold him up, he would be safe. The water—God himself—can hold you up and you can trust in that fact.

Let Go of Control and Meet Jesus

Let me state a truth: A lot of people are saved but they don't "know" Jesus. Of course they are saved by Jesus—our salvation is through faith in Christ alone—but they don't know him in the experiential or emotional sense of that word. That is the only way I can understand why people who believe and teach the doctrine of the sovereignty of God are so bent on controlling everything but him . . . and sometimes even him.

It is the only explanation I know for my condemnation, my arrogance, and my self-righteousness. It explains why people talk about freedom yet live in a prison of guilt and fear. It helps me deal with those who talk about grace and give very little of it. It is the only way I know to understand why I, a teacher of grace, live a life that is sometimes marked by obsession with rules, being perfect, and doing everything right. It explains why so many people have to be right and work so hard to appear to be good.

I don't for a moment believe that I'm not saved. (Contrary to what some of you think.) And frankly, I don't really believe that other Christians who drive me nuts with criticism and condemnation aren't redeemed. I just believe that I (and they) are saved but sometimes don't *know* Jesus.

You've probably heard of the facts/faith/feelings teaching about how to get feelings into line. There is something to that. The Christian faith really is based on facts. According to this view, once one determines those facts are true and behaves accordingly, the feelings follow. We already discussed that earlier in this minibook.

But what do you do if the feelings *don't* follow?

For many years, I followed Christ in a not dissimilar way to the way I followed the multiplication tables. I knew that it was true. It didn't move me deeply, it didn't make me "feel good all over," and it didn't feel "warm and fuzzy." During that period in my life, I simply didn't understand those who had an emotional connection with Christ. I, from my arrogant, self-righteous, and superficial position of intellectual commitment, felt that they "needed" all that, but all I needed was the truth.

After all, once you see truth, you can't unsee it. Only a fool, once seeing it, refuses to live according to the truth one has seen.

As I look back on it, the problem was that I tried to make the Christian faith into an affirmation of propositions. It was intellectual assent, and I thought that was enough. It wasn't—not nearly enough.

A man in Amherst, Massachusetts, proposed to his wife this way: "I hope I have no foolishness called romance; I am too well balanced for that sort of nonsense. But we might look forward to leading respectable and useful lives and enjoy the respect of the neighbors."

If you think that was good marriage proposal, there's something weird about you, and everybody knows it. But if you believe something like that about your relationship to Christ (the Lover of your soul) and even teach it, making the Christian faith into a "respectable and useful" religious commitment, everybody will think you're godly. You're not. You're just religious.

I know. I'm not preaching at you—I've been there and, God help me, still live there sometimes. It's having it in your head, but having trouble getting it into your heart.

I don't know if I have all the answers. I do have at least one of them though. If you sometimes have trouble getting what you know to be true into your heart, what follows might help.

With me, I think the real problem was (and sometimes still is) control. In my need to control my situation, my church, and all the circumstances of my life, I was saved but I didn't *know* Jesus. Jesus said about the scribes and Pharisees,

> "The scribes and the Pharisees sit on Moses' seat, so practice and observe whatever they tell you [i.e., they have the propositions and the doctrines right], but not what they do. . . . They tie up heavy burdens, hard to bear, and lay them on people's shoulders. . . . You [scribes and the Pharisees] shut the kingdom of heaven in people's faces. For you neither enter yourselves nor allow those who would enter to go in. . . . You travel across sea and land to make a single proselyte, and when he becomes a proselyte, you make him twice as much a child of hell as yourselves." (Matthew 23:2–4, 13–15)

You see, you can analyze, teach, and line up doctrines and propositions. There is something logical and proper about biblical theology. Apologetics will not only win arguments, it can make one feel secure in one's "rightness."

On the other hand, what goes on inside us—in our hearts and emotions—can be quite wild and we can be afraid of that. Trusting your heart, listening to your heart, and acting on your heart's "reasons" can get you into all sorts of trouble. Once you start going down the road of the heart, you can't control what happens. Not only that, there is something . . . well . . . uh . . . you know . . . kind of crude about all that emotional stuff.

Am I saying that biblical doctrine isn't of any consequence? Am I suggesting that what Francis Schaeffer called "true truth" isn't true or, if it is, it isn't all that important? Do I think that the eternal verities of the Christian faith are to be subjugated by the "things of the heart"? Of course not!

I am, however, saying that all of those things have one purpose: to point you to Christ so that he will love you and empower you to love, serve, and enjoy him. And loving, serving, and enjoying God are all things that start from a heart attached to God by faith.

Do you remember when you first learned to drive a car? If you're an old guy like me, you learned on a manual transmission. Do you remember all the hassle you had in changing the gears without stalling the car? Do you remember being at a stoplight on a steep hill and wondering how in the world you were going to get your foot off the brake and onto the clutch fast enough to keep from slipping back into the car behind you? Do you remember the efforts at keeping the car between the lines, not weaving? Do you remember trying to stop at stop signs and to start when the light turned green without looking like a fool riding a camel?

Were all those things important to learn? Of course they were. Somewhere along the line, though, you learned to drive without always thinking about the clutch, about the laws, and about keeping the car in the right lane. Those things became a part of you. If they didn't, you are probably miserable every time you drive a car. If "doing it right" is still how you drive the car, you never enjoy the scenery or listen to music. You are never able to relax. It takes all you've got to do it right. Once driving became a part of you, though, you were free to drive.

Let me give you some wonderful words from Jesus to think about.

> As they were going along the road, someone said to him, "I will follow you wherever you go." And Jesus said to him, "Foxes have holes, and birds of the air have nests, but the Son of Man has nowhere to lay his head." To another he said, "Follow me." But he said, "Lord, let me first go and bury my father." And Jesus said to him, "Leave the dead to bury their own dead. But as

for you, go and proclaim the kingdom of God." Yet another said, "I will follow you, Lord, but let me first say farewell to those at my home." Jesus said to him, "No one who puts his hand to the plow and looks back is fit for the kingdom of God." (Luke 9:57–62)

Jesus isn't teaching that there is something wrong with caring about having a "place to lay your head," about burying your relatives, or about taking care of your loved ones. Jesus is talking about control. He is calling you (and me too!) to let go of everything we are trying to have, hold, and control, and just follow him.

Of course, we aren't going to let go of the control of anything until we can trust the One to whom we are giving control. And that's why I'm always saying things like *God isn't angry at you. He is quite fond of you. He isn't a child abuser. Go to him and he won't reject you. He's not surprised at anything you do. It isn't your sin; it's your stiffness. If you never get any better, he will still love you.*

How do I know all that? Well, of course, I know that because the Bible tells me so. I don't really know it until I test it, though, and I have over and over again. Go ahead and test it.

Make a fool of yourself at church; laugh at an inappropriate time; dance in a Presbyterian church;

shout "Amen" in the middle of the Anglican liturgy; admit you're wrong to someone who really ticks you off; offend someone with your views; love someone nobody else can stand; do something improper; cuss, spit, and . . . okay, okay, maybe that is a bit much. You get the idea. Quit trying to be so right, so good, and so . . . well . . . in control. You're covered by the blood of Christ. The stiffness (i.e., your trying to get it right, be good, and never, ever let anyone see you sweat) will kill you.

You and Jesus can't both be in control. When I've tried to be in control, he still loved me and I was saved, but it felt like he was avoiding me. When I clung to my doctrines and my need to be right, good, and in control, Jesus allowed me to do that (although of course he was the one really in control the whole time!). However, when I decided that I didn't have to be in control anymore and, as it were, "let the dead bury their dead," I found that Jesus came and spoke to my heart deeply and profoundly.

Not only that—when was the last time you were hugged by or danced with a doctrine . . . no matter how true it was?

But Jesus, a friend of sinners, will hug you and dance with you. Give him your plans, your life, your heart, your mind, your present, past, and future. When believing is hard, ask him to help you. He promises that he stands at the door of your heart and knocks. Swing wide the door and let him in. You will never be disappointed by him.

Endnotes

1.   Lewis Carroll, *Through the Looking Glass, and What Alice Found There* (New York: MacMillan, 1897), Google Books e-book, 100.

Are you tired of
"do more, try harder" religion?

Key Life has only one message, to communicate the radical grace of God to sinners and sufferers. Because of what Jesus has done, God's not mad at you.

··

··

On radio, in print, on CDs and online, we're proclaiming the scandalous reality of Jesus' good news of radical grace…leading to radical freedom, infectious joy and surprising faithfulness to Christ.

For all things grace, visit us at **KeyLife.org**